CW00841413

GCSE REV: NOTES F __ CHARLES DICKENS'S *A CHRISTMAS CAROL* - Study guide (All staves, page-by-page analysis)

by Joe Broadfoot

ISBN-13: 978-1514126189

ISBN-10: 1514126184

Brief Introduction

This book is aimed at GCSE students of English Literature who are studying Charles Dickens's *A Christmas Carol*. The focus is on what examiners are looking for and here you will find each chapter covered in detail. I hope this will help you and be a valuable tool in your studies and revision.

Criteria for high marks

Make sure you use appropriate critical language (see glossary of literary terms at the back). You need your argument to be fluent, well-structured and coherent. Stay focused!

Analyse and explore the use of form, structure and the language. Explore how these aspects affect the meaning.

Make connections between texts and look at different interpretations. Explore their strengths and weaknesses. Don't forget to use supporting references to strengthen your argument.

Analyse and explore the context.

Best essay practice

Use PEE for your paragraphs: point/evidence/explain.

Other tips

Make your studies active!

Don't just sit there reading! Never forget to annotate, annotate and annotate!

All page references refer to the 2003 edition of *A Christmas Carol And Other Christmas Writings* published by Penguin Books (ISBN-13: 978-0-140-43905-2 & EISBN-978-0-141-93473-0).

A Christmas Carol

AQA (New specification starting in 2015)

If you're studying for an AQA qualification in English Literature, there's a good chance your teachers will choose this text to study. There are good reasons for that: it's moralistic and familiar to students. The text encourages us to think about right and wrong.

However, one of the difficulties is the language. That can't be helped, bearing in mind that part A of the exam paper involves answering questions on Shakespeare, whereas part B is all about the 19th-century novel.

To further complicate things, the education system is in a state of flux: that means we have to be ready for constant change. Of course, everyone had got used to grades A,B and C meaning a pass. It was simple, it was straightforward and nearly everyone understood it. Please be prepared that from this day henceforward, the top grade will now be known as 9. A grade 4 will be a pass, and anything below that will be found and anything above it will be a pass. Hopefully, that's not too confusing for anyone!

Now onto the exam itself. As I said, paper 1 consists of Shakespeare and the 19th-century novel. It is a written closed book exam (in other words you are not allowed to have the texts with you), which lasts one hour 45 minutes. You can score 64 marks, which amounts to 40% of your GCSE grade. The other 60% is gained from paper 2, which is all about modern texts, poetry and unseen poetry. But enough about paper 2, as our concern here is paper 1 and more specifically section B: the 19th-century novel.

In section B, students will be expected to write in detail about an extract from the novel they have studied in class and then write about the novel as a whole. In the case of *A Christmas Carol*, technically speaking it's a novella: or in other words, something longer than a short story but shorter than a novel. The fact that it is less worthy than some of the other texts available to study also makes it a popular choice with students.

Just for the record, the other choices of novel are the following: *The Strange Case of Dr Jekyll and Mr Hyde* by Robert Louis Stevenson, *Great Expectations* by Charles Dickens, *Jane Eyre* by Charlotte Brontë, *Frankenstein* by Mary Shelley, *Pride and Prejudice* by Jane Austin, and The Sign of Four by Sir Arthur Conan Doyle. Of course, all the above novels are well worth a read, but for our purposes we will simply concentrate on *A Christmas Carol* by Charles Dickens.

Another important thing to consider is the fact that for section B of paper 1, you will not be assessed on assessment objective 4 (AO4), which involves spelling, punctuation, grammar and vocabulary. This will be assessed on section A of paper 1, which is about Shakespeare, and it will be worth 2.5% of your overall GCSE grade. In terms of raw marks, it is worth 4 out of 64. So for once, we need not concern ourselves with what is affectionately known as 'SPAG' too much.

However, it is necessary to use the correct literary terminology wherever possible to make sure we maximise our marks on assessment objective2 (AO2). AO2 tests how well we can analyse language form and structure. Additionally, we are expected to state the effect the writer tried to create and how it impacts on the reader.

This brings me onto assessment objective 1 (AO1), which involves you writing a personal response to the text. It is important that you use quotations to backup your points of view. Like AO2, AO1 is worth 15% of your GCSE on Paper 1.

Assessment objective 3 (AO3) is worth half of that, but nevertheless it is important to comment on context to make sure you get as much of the 7.5% up for grabs as you can.

So just to make myself clear, there are 30 marks available in section B for your answer on the 19th-century novel. Breaking it down even further, you will get 12 marks maximum the backing up your personal opinion with quotations, an additional 12 marks for analysing the writer's choice of words for effect (not forgetting to use appropriate terminology -

more on that see the glossary at the back of this book), and six marks for discussing context.

As you can see, we've got a lot to get through so without further ado let's get on with the actual text itself and possible exam questions.

Previous exam questions

Notwithstanding the governmental changes to the grading system, it is still good practice to go over previous exam papers. I'm looking at a specimen paper from 2014, which asks students to read an extract from stave 1, which begins: 'External heat and cold had little influence on Scrooge' (p34). It ends with: 'To edge his way along the crowded parts of life, warning all human sympathy to keep its distance, was what the knowing ones call 'nuts' to Scrooge' (35).

Students are expected to read the extract and comment about how Dickens presents Scrooge as an outsider to society. Students should say how that is shown in the extract itself and also on the whole novel. Despite the changes to the syllabus, future questions are likely to be very similar. Of course, it could be about a different character, but it will involve looking at the extract for the first part of the question and then moving on to discuss the whole novel. That's the format and is unlikely to change in the near future. So no worries there then! [SEE FULL ANSWER TO THIS QUESTION FROM A SPECIMEN PAPER AFTER THE PAGE-BY-PAGE ANALYSIS.]

To make sure that you meet AQA's learning objectives and get a high mark, make sure you go into the exam knowing something about the following:

- the plot

- the characters

- the theme

- selected quotations/details

- exam skills

Now, we will be going through each of those objectives in turn, so you should be well prepared for the exam itself.

Basic plot

Okay, let's not have any silly jokes about losing the plot; instead let me ask you to rearrange these events in *A Christmas Carol.* You should be able to try it even if you haven't read the text yet.

Event A: Scrooge wakes up on Christmas morning, after a restless night involving visitations of ghosts.

Event B: The chained ghost of Jacob Marley visits Scrooge, telling him that he will be visited by three more ghosts and warning them to modify his behaviour or face the same fate.

Event C: The Ghost Of Christmas Present warns Scrooge that Tiny Tim will die should nothing change.

Event D: Scrooge sees his own death thanks to The Ghost Of Christmas Yet To Come. No one mourns him.

Event E: Scrooge gets into the spirit of Christmas, sending the Cratchits a turkey and joining Fred, his nephew, for a Christmas party. The reformed Scrooge dedicates his life to helping the poor and Tiny Tim does not die.

Event F: Scrooge is in a fearful mood, especially bearing in mind it's Christmas Eve and a time of goodwill to all. It really goes against the grain. He is rude to everyone he encounters especially his clerk, Bob Cratchit

Event G: The Ghost Of Christmas Yet To Come shows Scrooge the Cratchits mourning Tiny Tim's death.

Event H: Scrooge sees the Cratchits enjoying their Christmas party despite their abject poverty, thanks to the Ghost Of Christmas Present.

Event I: Scrooge sees scenes from his past, including the moment when his engagement with his fiancee was broken off. This was shown to him by the ghost of Christmas past.

Now let's make sure that he got that in the right order. Here is the **correct sequence** of events:

1. Event F: Scrooge is in a fearful mood, especially bearing in mind it's Christmas Eve and a time of goodwill to all. It really goes against the grain. He is rude to everyone he encounters especially his clerk, Bob Cratchit

2. Event B: The chained ghost of Jacob Marley visits Scrooge, telling him that he will be visited by three more ghosts and warning them to modify his behaviour or face the same fate.

3. Event I: Scrooge sees scenes from his past, including the moment when his engagement with his fiancee was broken off. This was shown to him by the ghost of Christmas past.

4. Event H: Scrooge sees the Cratchits enjoying their Christmas party despite their abject poverty, thanks to the Ghost Of Christmas Present.

5. Event C: The Ghost Of Christmas Present warns Scrooge that Tiny Tim will die should nothing change.

6. Event D: Scrooge sees his own death thanks to The Ghost Of Christmas Yet To Come. No one mourns him.

7. Event G: The Ghost Of Christmas Yet To Come shows Scrooge the Cratchits mourning Tiny Tim's death.

8. Event A: Scrooge wakes up on Christmas morning, after a restless night involving visitations of ghosts.

9. Event E: Scrooge gets into the spirit of Christmas, sending the Cratchits a turkey and joining Fred, his nephew, for a Christmas party. The reformed Scrooge dedicates his life to helping the poor and Tiny Tim does not die.

How many did you get right? If you get all of them, try again later.

Arguably, the most important aspect of those events are what happens at the end. Charles Dickens wanted political reform, in that he felt the rich were becoming richer without little regard for the poor and the terrible conditions that they lived in. The very fact that Scrooge, a rich man, becomes a reformed character is a political message to 19th-century society that they should try to emulate this newborn philanthropist. If you can write something like the above in an exam situation, should it be relevant to the question of course, you will score high marks for assessment objective 3 (AO3).

Other things to note about the context of the novella is there it was written in 1843, just nine years after the new Poor Law was introduced. This controversial piece of legislation meant that workhouses were set up in every parish. We must remember that in the 19th century there was no welfare state. If somebody lost a job, they would be reliant on relations or their own personal savings to survive. If they were poor and had nobody to take care of them, then they would have to go to the workhouse where conditions were horrific. In the workhouse, if a child was aged over seven they were not allowed to have any contact with the opposite sex; that meant young boys could not even talk to their sisters or mothers. The same in reverse applied to young girls. However, conditions were even worse for orphaned children, who were sent out of the workhouse as soon as possible to sweep chimneys or work in mines, usually. Again, applying contextual details such as these will get you marks for assessment objective 3 (AO3).

Now let's look more closely at the **structure** of the novella. It is split into staves, which is a rather interesting variation on chapters. Of course, given the musical title, it makes sense to use musical terminology like staves. There are five lines in a stave and that corresponds to how Dickens divides his story up into five parts.

Page-by-page analysis

Please note, some pages are illustrated by John Leech and are not analysed as we're looking at Dickens's writing here.

Stave One

Before stave one begins, there is a brief preface. I don't intend to dwell on it very much, aside from saying that Dickens lays out his idea to hold houses 'pleasantly'. By addressing the audience thus, the author achieves an intimate tone with his readers.

Stave one is entitled: 'Marley's Ghost'. Much is made of the fact that 'Marley was dead: to begin with' (p33). Indeed these are the opening words of the novella, such is their importance. The next most important part of the opening is the **simile**, 'Old Marley was as dead as a door nail' (33) This **foreshadows** what is about to happen, as Marley's ghost first appears on a door knocker, making the simile particularly apt.

Another striking aspect of the opening is the repetition of the word 'sole' (33). This emphasises how alone Scrooge is. There is even a mention of Hamlet's father, which foreshadows the fact that Marley's ghost is about to appear.

Dickens uses one of his famous lists to describe Scrooge, as 'a squeezing, wrenching, grasping, scraping, clutching, covetous old sinner! (34)' These adjectives in their -ing form show that Scrooge is continuing to behave in the manner and thus described.

A couple of similes show us even more about Scrooge's nature. He is described as 'hard and sharp as flint, from which no steel had ever struck out generous fire'. This shows how cold he is as a person and difficult to deal with.

We also discover that he is 'as solitary as an oyster' (34). No doubt he is as difficult to prise open, but inside the cold shell there is inside something of value. This suggests that deep inside Scrooge may not be quite as harsh as his exterior seems to suggest.

Scrooge is even negatively compared to the weather, which often '" came down" handsomely' (34). While the weather gives us unwelcome gifts like snow and rain, by contrast Scrooge is reluctant to give anything at all. He is a miser in the truest sense of the word.

We also discover that Scrooge is cold in every sense of the word. His thin lips are 'blue' and he ices his office between 3 July and 11 August ('the dog-days') to make sure he maintains his temperature, which seems to reflect his temperament (34).

Scrooge relishes the fact that people and blind men's dogs keep out of his way. For him, it is 'nuts', which is to say it is something agreeable.

More foreshadowing takes place, as we discover that this Christmas Eve, it is 'cold, bleak, biting' and 'foggy' (35). Some teachers would describe this as pathetic fallacy, so presumably some markers will consider it as that as well. There is an absence of light, which reflects Scrooge's dark personality. We find him 'sat busy in his counting house', presumably counting his money (35).

Meanwhile, we encounter Scrooge's clerk, Bob Cratchit, for the first time. He spends his time 'in a dismal little cell beyond, a sort of tank' (35). Bob's fire is even smaller than Scrooge's. We already feel some sympathy for this character, who wears a 'white comforter' to keep warm (35).

Shortly after that, we hear Scrooge's nephew, Fred, for the first time. Fred is the eternal optimist. Although Scrooge has no time for Christmas, Fred is the exact opposite. Fred is described as 'ruddy and handsome' (35). Indeed, Fred's point of view seems to mirror Dickens's, especially when he says that Christmas is a time to 'thinking people below [...] As if they really were fellow-passengers to the grave, and not another race of creatures bound on other journeys' (36). Fred seems to be preaching Dickens's own philosophy.

Fred refuses to give up on Scrooge, imploring his uncle to join him for Christmas dinner. Scrooge replies that he would rather see him damned first. Before he leaves, Fred wishes Bob a merry Christmas, which further infuriates his uncle Scrooge. In his rage, Scrooge reveals that Bob is only paid 'fifteen shillings' a week (37). A shilling is worth five pence in modern day money, but of course the cost of living has changed dramatically since the 19th century. However, bearing in mind that this novella cost five shillings upon its release in December 1843, you can understand that Bob Cratchit would have only been able to buy three copies.

As Fred leaves, two 'portly gentleman' come in. They are collecting for charity and Scrooge gives them short shrift. Scrooge mentions that 'union workhouses' are an option for poor people (38). Scrooge even refers to 'the treadmill' and the Poor Law' (38). The treadmill was a wheel that people would step on to pump water or produce grain; it was often used as a form of punishment in prisons and workhouses. Indeed, conditions in the workhouse was so poor that it literally was a last resort for people down on their luck. The 1834 Poor Law Amendment Act had resulted in many new workhouses being set up to cater for the poor. Dickens was vigourously opposed to this development, as he thought it robbed people of their dignity. As we can see, Scrooge at this stage in the novella represents the direct opposite to Dickens's political point of view.

Another political viewpoint that Dickens was against involved Malthusian economics. Once again, the view that Dickens was most opposed to, which was that population needed to be decreased by whatever means necessary. There was huge fears about the impact and consequences of overpopulation in England. These fears went right back to the 18th century, when Thomas Malthus wrote about that very subject. Here, Scrooge is Malthus's mouthpiece when he says that people dying in prisons and workhouses will 'decrease the surplus population' (39).

Meanwhile, the setting is almost literally caving in on Scrooge, with 'the fog and darkness' thickening (39). Through pathetic fallacy, the writer suggests that Scrooge cannot see the metaphorical light of truth at all; he is deluding himself.

Perhaps his God has not deserted him yet, as we see there is a 'gruff old bell' in an 'ancient tower of the church' which is 'always peeping slily down' (39). Through the use of personification, the writer shows that outside forces are at work on Scrooge and his disposition.

The fog not only persist but gets worse, as does Scrooge's behaviour. Now he forces a carol singer to flee 'in terror' from his wrath (40). Scrooge is now verging on violent and dangerous, so furious is he with the concept of Christmas.

However, Scrooge does allow Bob to take the day off on Christmas Day. He reminds him that he must be at work 'all the earlier next morning', which is, of course, Boxing Day (41). Back then, in 1843, Boxing Day was not a public holiday. We see Bob running home to Camden Town 'as hard as he could pelt', which shows us how enthusiastic he was about the Christmas season (41).

In direct contrast, we see Scrooge taking 'his melancholy dinner in his usual melancholy tavern' (41). This shows how alone Scrooge is and how miserable, as even in a sociable place like a tavern, Scrooge is solitary.

What follows is a description of Marley's face in Scrooge's doorknocker (42). The most remarkable thing about this description is this simile 'like a bad lobster in a dark cellar'.

Back in those days, there were no fridges, so many people kept perishable food in cellars; these were the coldest places in a house, generally. If a lobster had been kept too long and was no longer fresh, it would start to glow in the dark. We now know this is because of luminous photo bacteria. Like a bad lobster, Marley's death seven years ago means his body is certainly not fresh. We can read a lot into the comparison with a lobster, but ultimately probably only means that Marley had an eerie glow about him (as well he might given that he is a ghost).

Scrooge tries to put this vision behind him, but he is affected by it nonetheless. His motto is 'darkness is cheap', so Scrooge won't like any more candles despite what he has just seen (43). Nevertheless, he is more suspicious than usual, which improves when he double locks himself in, which is 'not his custom' (43).

When Scrooge finally sees all of Marley's ghost, and not just the face, he notices the chain made up of 'cash boxes, keys, padlocks, ledgers, deeds, and heavy purses wrought in steel' (44). His former business partner is literally a victim of miserly lifestyle. In death, Marley is condemned to be attached to things that have monetary value but no spiritual significance.

Despite Marley's ghost's fierce looks, Scrooge's initial attitude is light-hearted. For instance, 'Scrooge had often heard it said that Marley had no bowels' (44). This is a pun, as 'no bowels' meant 'no mercy'. However, Marley's ghost literally has no bowels as he is 'transparent' (44).

Scrooge continues to joke, telling Marley's ghost that he is 'particular - for shade' (45). Scrooge is trying to take control of the situation, even telling the ghost to sit down if you can. Scrooge then tries to dismiss the vision as a bit of 'undigested' food (45). He even says: 'There's more of gravy than of grave about you' (45).

However, Scrooge is mortified when the ghost literally creates a jaw-dropping moment, allowing its lower jaw to drop down 'upon its breast' (47). The spectre tell Scrooge of its woe: that 'cannot share' what it 'might have shared on earth' (47).

The ghost tells Scrooge that his chain will be even longer and more 'ponderous' than his is (48). Interestingly, Scrooge's reaction is to 'put his hands in his breeches pockets', as was his custom when he became thoughtful (48). It is almost as if he thinks he is being robbed, or is about to be robbed by the ghost. This shows his financial insecurity, and proves he's not listening fully to the warnings he is being given. He's more mindful of money than anything else.

There is light imagery to consider when the ghost relates how he can't raise his eyes 'to that blessed Star which led the Wise Men to a poor abode' (49). Of course, this is a biblical reference to the birth of Jesus and the three wise men following a star to find Christ's birthplace. The implication here is that Scrooge has a chance to see the light, before it's too late as in the case of Marley.

The ghost tells Scrooge exactly what to expect. Scrooge will see three more ghosts, the first arriving at 1am on Christmas

Day. The second will arrive at the same time on Boxing Day, while the third will be due 'when the last stroke of twelve has ceased to vibrate' on 27th of December (50). Obviously, as you will find out when you read on, the ghosts do not rigidly stick to the schedule. This may suggest that Scrooge has dreamt the whole thing, and the supernatural does not exist. It is certainly one interpretation, but not the only one.

Scrooge gets round to looking out the window after Marley's ghost drifts out of it, and there he sees many other ghosts. The narrator says 'some few (they might be guilty governments) were linked together (52). This reminds the reader that the story has a very strong political message, as Dickens blamed the various governments for the treatment of the poor.

Stave Two

Stave two is entitled: 'The First Of The Three Spirits'. In its opening, we immediately discover that Scrooge is still concerned about his financial situation, as he is worried that some people who owe him money may default on their loans, a bit like 'a mere United States' security' (53). Indeed, this happened in 1837, when some American states borrow money from English capitalists, but could not pay it back due to a financial crisis.

We finally get to see 'a strange figure - like a child' (54). Clearly, we will venture into Scrooge's childhood with this ghost. However, the past is not always remembered clearly, which may be why the ghost is also 'like an old man' (55). This represents indistinct memories of the past. The most significant thing about this ghost is 'that from the crown of its head there sprung a bright clear jet of light' (55). This shows us that the ghost wants to illuminate the past for Scrooge to learn lessons from it. As well as that, the ghost has 'a great extinguisher for a cap', which of course was nothing like a fire extinguisher, but more a device for putting out a candle (55).

This cap is very significant as a ghost accuses Scrooge of making him 'wear it low upon' his brow (56). Scrooge denies this allegation, he wouldn't have 'bonneted' the ghost wilfully (56). Bonneting was considered loutish behaviour, in the 19th century, so Scrooge would be highly unlikely to indulge in this activity given his economic and social status. However, it does allude to his hidden childish nature perhaps.

We soon see Scrooge as 'a solitary child, neglected by his friends' at Christmas time (57). This arouses the reader sympathy for Scrooge, for perhaps the first time. It also explains some of his negative and antisocial behaviour.

The next image we see of Scrooge shows him as 'a lonely boy' (58). This time he is 'reading near a feeble fire', which is almost reminiscent of Bob's situation in his tank in Scrooge's office (58). Scrooge uses his imagination to cheer himself up, just like he did when he was a boy, by describing a foreign gentleman he sees outside as 'Ali Baba' (58). The young Scrooge is clearly comforting himself with characters from novels to make up for the lack of real people in his life. Again this evokes sympathy from the reader.

After these visions of the past, Scrooge begins to regret his behaviour with the carol singer. He tells the ghost: I should like to have given him something: that's all' (59). This shows that Scrooge has the intention to change his ways.

We then see Scrooge's younger sister being very affectionate to him and inviting him home for Christmas. She tells him: 'home's like Heaven!' (60). Once again, the reader feels sorry for Scrooge who clearly has had a difficult home life.

The next vision is far more cheerful. Scrooge gets to see his old employer, Fezziwig, who is rather a large 'jovial' man (61). Phrenology was a very popular pseudoscience at the time, and the narrator mentions Fezziwig's 'organ of benevolence', which suggests that his forehead may be the reason for his kindness.

The author uses synecdoche in describing Mrs Fezziwig as 'one vast substantial smile'. In a short phrase, the writer has successfully conveyed the idea that she is full of the joys of life. In a novella or short story, there simply isn't the time to put flesh on the bones of some characters. Therefore, like her husband, Mrs Fezziwig remains a stock character.

These two are extremely effective in cheering up others. So much so that 'a positive light' appears 'to issue from Fezziwig's calves' (63). They shine 'like moons' (63). Through the use of a simile and light imagery, Dickens can effectively convey the idea that Fezziwig is a merry old soul.

The ghost and Scrooge discuss Fezziwig, with the former calling the party they have just witnessed 'a small matter'

(64). Scrooge cannot agree with that perspective. The ghost goes on to say that Fezziwig 'has spent than a few pounds of your mortal money' (64). Scrooge then conveys a sentiment much closer to that of the author, when he replies: 'The happiness he gives, is quite as great as if it cost a fortune' (64).

We now see Scrooge as 'a man in the prime of life' (65). His 'eager, greedy' and restless ways have got the better of his better nature. He is accused by his former fiancee, Belle, as being obsessed with 'Gain' (65). The word is personified by the capital letter, suggesting that it is so powerful that it almost speaks to him. She says that she hoped they would improve their fortunes with 'patient industry', another way of saying hard work (65). This is a sentiment that Dickens would be likely to approve of. Similarly, most readers of the time would warm to Scrooge's fiancee.

Before Scrooge's fiancee leaves him, she mentions only may recall their time together as 'an unprofitable dream' (66). Of course, profit is everything to Scrooge, and if he can dismiss what the ghosts are telling him as figments of his imagination and dreamlike state, then he is unlikely to learn any lessons at all.

The ghost now takes Scrooge forward in time to see his ex-fiancee's family set up. She is now 'a comely matron' and everything is domestic bliss (67). This is in direct contrast to Scrooges lonely lifestyle, which makes his situation seem all the more miserable.

Just to make sure that the reader can see the contrast, Belle's husband describes Scrooge as: 'Quite alone in the world' (68). At this point, Marley was about to die, so Scrooge had no one to turn to. Again, the reader may feel a little more sympathy for Scrooge's predicament. The writer appears to be building up Scrooge as a sympathetic character very subtly and slowly.

However, Scrooge is not reformed character yet, as we see when he seizes the ghost's 'extinguisher-cap' and presses it 'down upon its head' (70). By doing that, Scrooge extinguishes the light and ends his chances of learning more from his past. Once again, he appears to be settling for darkness, which he seems more comfortable with.

Stave Three

Stave three is entitled: 'The Second Of The Three Spirits'. We get the idea very quickly that Scrooge is ready for anything that spirits can throw at him. The narrator says: 'Nothing between a baby and a rhinoceros would have astonished him very much' (71).

What appears is a 'jolly Giant' (71). It brings abundance, sitting on a throne of food. It seems welcoming to Scrooge, holding aloft 'a glowing torch, in shape not unlike Plenty's horn' (71). Plenty is personified through the use of a capital letter, which adds to its importance. Clearly, Dickens felt there was plenty of food to go around, and enough to share with the poorer classes.

With Scrooge old habits die hard, for when the ghost tells him that he has 'more than eighteen hundred' brothers, the former replies that it is: 'A tremendous family to provide for' (74). Once again, Scrooge seems obsessed with the size of the population, rather like Thomas Malthus.

We then see people shovelling together to clear the snow in the present, and we discover how 'jovial and full of glee' they are (75). The community spirit of Christmas is evoked, and juxtaposed with Scrooge's solitary condition it shows how much is missing out on.

Using personification, and more particularly pathetic fallacy, Dickens shows the power of the church by having the steeples call 'good people all, to church' (76). By good people, Dickens means those who could afford to go to church, as not everyone could do that. For working classes, Sunday was the only day they could get a cooked meal, courtesy of a baker's oven. Dickens was vehemently opposed to the strict observance of Sunday as a day of rest and worship for this reason. The idea that Sundays should be reserved for churchgoing and prayer was advocated by the Sabbatarian Movement, who ignored the fact that the lower classes could only enjoy recreational activities on their only day off from work.

We then encounter 'dinner-carriers' jostling with each other and sometimes exchanging 'angry words', as the ghost and Scrooge watch on. The ghost has to 'shed a few drops of water on them' from his torch to make sure that 'good humour' is maintained (77). This shows how desperate poor people were to eat their hot Sunday dinner, on the only day of the week when they could. Dickens is showing how divine intervention, from the ghost in this case, makes people's lives better. The implication is that governments could do more to improve the lot of the suffering.

Soon after, Mrs Cratchit is described as 'brave in ribbons'. This shows how defiant she is to look her best, despite her family's lack of wealth. The writer describes her efforts as 'a goodly show for sixpence', which in old money was half a shilling or in today's money 2.5 pence. Again, the writer is showing poor people in a positive light. The political meaning beneath is that hard-working poor people should receive more money.

The Cratchit family are used by Dickens to revoke pathos in the reader. In particular, the alliteratively named Tiny Tim generates most sympathy, for he bears 'a little crutch' and has 'his limbs supported by a nine frame' (79). You will notice that Dickens often uses the word 'little' to describe Tiny Tim, whose very name indicates that the author wants us to feel sorry for this disabled character. Sometimes, Dickens is accused of being over-sentimental, but at the time using the suffering of a child was a popular formula to achieve more book sales. Given that it sold 5,000 copies in its first week, Dickens certainly achieved his ambition with his novella. Nevertheless, some modern-day readers find it distasteful that Dickens portrays a disabled character in such a way. A more modern version would be likely to portrays Tiny Tim as less helpless and more active, rather than just a passive victim. However, much of the pathos would be lost with such a portrayal.

Tiny Tim, according to his father, has quoted from the New Testament, which was Dickens's favourite part of the Bible. Referring to the miracle of healing performed by Christ, Bob relates to his family: 'He told me, coming home, that he hoped the people saw him in the church, because he was a cripple, and it might be pleasant to then to remember upon Christmas Day, who made lame beggars walk and blind men see' (80). These Christian ideas are important because they convey the message of hope. In the absence of Jesus, Dickens properly means that government intervention is needed to help poor suffering people.

The Cratchits are an example of how poor people try to make the most of what they have. Although they only have a goose to eat the Christmas, rather than a turkey, 'its tenderness and flavour, size and cheapness' are 'the themes of universal admiration' (81). Of course, by 'universal', the writer is only talking about the Cratchit family, so this is hyperbole for comic effect. However, extolling the virtue of 'cheapness' is an example of Victorian thrift. This would have been much lauded at the time especially, making the Cratchit family particularly appealing to the readers.

We get an even better picture of how close poor families can be when the Cratchit family draw 'round the heath' (82). This represents the idealised Victorian home, whereby all the family gathered around an open fire. There are even 'chestnuts on the fire' crackling 'noisily' evoking the spirit of Christmas and family love (82). Tiny Tim sits very close to his father, but the ghost says ominously that he sees 'a crutch without an owner, carefully preserved' (82). This shows

Scrooge that unless he changes his ways, Bob's disabled child will die. It also shows that the Cratchits will be distraught at the loss of Tiny Tim, but they will preserve his memory by looking after his crutch. Perhaps this kind of sentimentality works less well today with readers than it did in Dickens's time, but nonetheless the author effectively conveys the idea of unconditional family love.

There is an element of realism in the scene, however, as Mrs Cratchit has to be convinced by her husband to toast Scrooge. Bob implores her to raise a glass for 'The Founder of the Feast' (83). Even Tiny Tim baulks at this, as the narrator reveals that he didn't give 'twopence for' this toast (83). This gives us an idea of how all the family realise how exploited their father raised by Scrooge and his paltry wages.

We then see numerous other families getting together the Christmas. We witness 'the brightness of the roaring fires in kitchens, parlours, and all sorts of rooms' as the ghost lights the way in the darkness (84). Clearly, Scrooge has two see the light, metaphorically speaking, to change his ways.

The ghost takes Scrooge to 'a place where miners live', which proves even workers in the harshest conditions can enjoy Christmas (85). This is in stark contrast to Scrooge, who has money but cannot enjoy spending it. There is even more joy in 'a solitary lighthouse' then there is in Scrooge's quarters (85).

Finally, Scrooge gets to experience Christmas 'on a ship' and not surprisingly the sailors enjoy their celebrations. However, to Scrooge, it is 'a great surprise' to 'hear a hearty laugh' on-board a ship moving 'through the lonely darkness of an unknown abyss' (86).

We may exceed Fred and his wife discussing Scrooge. Although, Scrooge's niece-in-law has nothing good to say about Fred's uncle, her husband says: 'His offences carry their own punishment, and I have nothing to say against him' (87). By this, Fred is suggesting that Scrooge suffers most by being ill-tempered and is refusing to fight fire with fire. It is a very Christian sentiment and one in keeping with the Christmas spirit and Dickens's own point of view.

We now have a comic interlude, with Topper chasing one of Scrooge's niece's sisters. Topper does say that 'a bachelor was a wretched outcast', which suggests that Scrooge's inability to find a love match makes him unnatural (88). Indeed, we assume Scrooge has little or no experience of chasing women, as his sole purpose is to collect more money.

We then see more of what Scrooge is missing, as the party begin to play games. Topper takes his pursuit of Scrooge's niece's 'plump sister' to the extreme, cheating blind-man's buff in order to capture (89). Although this is cheating, it is all in good fun. This playful scene stands in direct contrast with the miserable and lonely life that Scrooge leads.

Indeed, Scrooge enjoys the games and atmosphere so much, he begs the spirit to let him stay longer 'until the guests departed' (90). However, the spirit says it cannot be done. Another lesson is to be learned from this, and even good times come to an end so we must take advantage of every opportunity that we can to have fun.

Scrooge just manages to witness a game of 'Yes and No', in which the guests have to guess what Scrooge's nephew is thinking of (90). Fred is only allowed to answer yes or no to their questions. Eventually, the guests discover that Fred is thinking of his uncle Scrooge. At that discovery, some object, saying: 'the reply to "Is it a bear?" ought to have been "Yes" (91). Presumably, the guests believe that Scrooge is like a bear with a sore head. Despite the insult, Scrooge is still 'light of heart' (91). This is evidence that he has undergone a fundamental change in his personality.

After leaving the party, Scrooge notices that 'a foot or claw' is protruding from underneath the spirit's rope (92). The ghost reveals a boy and a girl, who are described as 'yellow, meagre, ragged, scowling, wolfish; but prostrate, too, in their humility' (92). In short, they look more like devils than angels because their physical condition is so pitiful. The writer is reminding us that many evils are hidden, even during the time of rejoicing in the Christmas season.

In response to Scrooge's enquiry, the ghost names the boy as 'Ignorance' and the girl as 'Want' (94). The spirit says that the boy is to be most feared, as on his brow is written the word: 'Doom' (94). Obviously, the hidden meaning is that education can eradicate ignorance and therefore give poor children the opportunity to earn more money and provide better for their families. Dickens had already made steps to provide education for the poor by persuading his wealthy friend, Angela Burdette-Coutts, to help set up the Ragged Schools.

Stave four

This stave is entitled: The Last Of The Spirits. The narrative pace picks up considerably here and the tension increases partly because the final ghost is 'silent shape' (95). It only points in answer to Scrooge's questions, and the fear that the protagonist feels is conveyed effectively to the reader.

This ghost takes Scrooge to the Royal Exchange, where much of London's business is conducted. We see a typical Dickensian 'grotesque', as 'a red-faced gentleman with a pendulous excrescence on the end of his nose, that shook like the gills of the turkey-cock' enquires about what an unknown dead man has done with his money (96). Scrooge had seen these merchants before, and watches on as they discuss the death amongst themselves.

We discover that the mystery dead man, was nicknamed 'Old Scratch' after the devil (97). The reader can guess the identity of the dead man, but Scrooge hasn't fully realised it is him yet. Scrooge initially thinks that these conversations are 'trivial' (97). However, he does hope to discover the 'hidden purpose' behind the ghost insisting that he witnesses these (97). Maybe this shows Scrooge is not quite educated enough to become a reformed character yet. Perhaps it also shows that he is still naïve, and for that reason some readers may have sympathy for him.

Additionally, some readers may feel sympathy for Scrooge's fear of the phantom. This description of the 'Unseen Eyes' 'looking at him keenly' makes the silent ghost look all the more menacing (98).

More threatening still are the metaphorical vultures, masquerading as human beings, plundering the dead man of all his possessions. The ghost takes Scrooge to see old Joe's parlour. In it, 'the charwoman', 'the laundress' and 'the undertaker's man' all take the chance to sell what they found on the body of the dead man (99).

We find out exactly what the dead man is worth. The first metaphorical vulture opens a bundle to reveal 'a seal or two, a pencil-case, a pair of sleeve-buttons, and a brooch of no great value' (100). This is all that the charwoman, Mrs Dilber's friend has been able to produce. At this stage, it doesn't seem like that deceased was a very rich man, which may encourage Scrooge to believe it is not him.

Mrs Dilber's haul is even less impressive. She produces 'sheets and towels, a little wearing apparel, two old-fashioned silver teaspoons, a pair of sugar-tongs, and a few boots' (100). This suggests so far, how meagre the monetary value is of those things left behind.

Mrs Dilber's friend has a bundle of her own, but all that is contained within are 'bed-curtains' (101). She seems the more mercenary of the two, which is a recipe for success in these days of unflinching and unmerciful capitalism.

Scrooge is mortified by 'this dialogue', viewing them with 'detestation and disgust' (102). The ominous signs are there, but Scrooge refuses to recognise them despite the phantom pointing 'to the head' of the deceased (102). Scrooge is still not ready to accept the truth.

This bleak scene is made in the worse by sound imagery, as we discover 'a cat' is 'tearing at the door' and there is a 'sound of Noreen rats beneath a hearth-stone' (103). It is almost as if these animals will be eating the dead man's corpse in the not too distant future.

The ghost then takes Scrooge to people that feel emotion at the dead man's death. We discover that for this 'care-worn and depressed' young husband' 'there is hope yet' (103, 104). The reason he and his wife Caroline are going to sleep better than usual, is because their debt will be transferred to an alive debt collector, instead of the dead man. This is a very cynical but realistic view of how some people view death.

Much less cynical is what follows, Scrooge and the ghost view Mrs Cratchit blaming 'her work' on her 'eyes', which are presumably leaking tears (105). To make the pathos more effective in the scene, Bob Cratchit appears to be very cheerful, despite the death of his son (105). This technique would work particularly well with 19th-century readers, who were less inclined to be cynical when it comes to sentiment.

Bob tries to keep his stiff upper lip, but fails to do so breaking 'down all at once' (106). This shows our human he is. Bob does his best to compose himself, by sitting down in the bedroom of his recently departed son. He even kisses 'the little face' (106). Bob has found his own way of dealing with death, which wouldn't be so uncommon during Victorian times.

Despite seeing all of this, Scrooge is still preoccupied with the mystery dead man. He implored the ghost to tell him 'what man that was whom we saw lying dead?' (107). The question is at this stage, is he just curious or is he selfish? It is a little strange that he has no comment to make about Tiny Tim's death. Surely this doesn't make the reader sympathise with more, as Scrooge seems only concerned with himself.

We discover in this over populated cemetery, that the 'neglected' gravestone indeed bears the name: 'EBENEZER SCROOGE' (108). There is no doubt at all by now that Scrooge will die unless he changes his life.

Scrooge pledges to 'honour Christmas' in his 'heart, and try to keep it all the year' (110). This in effect means that Scrooge will make every day like Christmas. He has finally decided to changes character completely.

Stave five

This stave is entitled: The End Of It. It is largely concerned with Scrooge making the best that he can run one single day. He is described 'as making a perfect Laocoon of himself', which refers to the Trojan priest who was right to try to convince his fellow countrymen from dragging the Trojan horse into Troy (111). Laocoon was unfortunate enough to be killed by divine intervention, yet we assume that a different fate awaits Scrooge.

Scrooge admits that he is 'quite a baby', without a care in the world (112). This shows that the author is trying to get the readers to openly admit to having a more infantile side, which is altogether more in keeping with nature.

In keeping with this mood, Scrooge orders and incredulous boy to 'go and buy' a turkey for Bob Cratchit's family (113). Scrooge is showing that action speaks louder than words, by effectively putting his money where his mouth is.

To make up for lost time, Scrooge encounters 'the portly gentleman', who had been collecting money to charity the day before (114). Scrooge makes a generous donation, whispering in the portly gentleman's 'ear', so we as readers are only left to guess how much he's contributing to the cause (114).

Soon there is plenty of repetition, as Scrooge finds himself at Fred's party. It is described as 'a wonderful party' with 'wonderful games, wonderful unanimity' and wonder-ful happiness!' (115). Clearly, the author is waxing lyrical about how beneficial a social occasion such as this is to everyone involved.

Scrooge is so pleased that he is now in the mood to make a joke with his employee, Bob Cratchit. The poor man is 'eighteen minutes and a half' late for work. Scrooge says that he is 'not going to stand this sort of thing any longer' (116). At this point, Bob thinks he's losing his job. However, Scrooge clarifies the situation telling him he is about 'to raise' his 'salary' (116). The author is clearly trying to get across the idea that Christmas is a time of goodwill to all men.

Dickens ends with a pun in his last paragraph writing that Scrooge 'and no further intercourse with Spirits, but lived upon the Total Abstinence Principle' (118). The author is indicating that rather than avoiding alcohol, Scrooge will be avoiding ghosts. This is a rather clever ending to the novella.

Sample essay question

The AQA specimen paper from 2014 asks students to read an extract from stave 1, which begins: 'External heat and cold had little influence on Scrooge' (p34). It ends with: 'To edge his way along the crowded parts of life, warning all human sympathy to keep its distance, was what the knowing ones call 'nuts' to Scrooge' (35).

Students are expected to read the extract and comment about how Dickens presents Scrooge as an outsider to society. Students should say how that is shown in the extract itself and also on the whole novel.

Okay first things first, let's look at the question. The keywords are: 'outsider to society'. So to reiterate, we must look through the extract first to find examples of where Scrooge appears to be an outsider. Then we need to think of examples in the text as a whole.

At this stage, we need to concentrate on AO2, which deals with language, form and structure. If possible we need to use literary terms to describe the language that Dickens uses and of course we need to comment on the effects. If we can do that, we can score maximum of 12 marks. The same applies to AO1, which concerns our personal response. Finally, if we can insert some comments about context we can score maximum six marks for those comments.

Details in the extract showing Scrooge as an outsider

First of all, we need to decide what an outsider is. My definition for the purposes of this question is: a person who does not fraternise or socialise with others and is uncaring as he keeps himself to himself.

I will begin my answer with notes, starting at the top of the extract and going right down to the bottom of it:

1. 'External heat and cold had little influence on Scrooge' (34) - this shows his different to most people, and therefore strange and possibly an outsider.

AO1: Personal response: The reader may think that Scrooge is weird and certainly cold, and it is this latter were warm heart and makes him an outsider.

AO2: The writer's effect: The writer uses the word 'external' which shows the reader that Scrooge is living in a shell. His outside is impenetrable. This foreshadows what is about to happen, as we find out later that Scrooge has a soft centre. However he is a hard nut to crack.

AO3: Context - not applicable.

2. 'No wind that blew was bitterer than he' (34) - this shows Scrooge is bitter at society and unsociable. However, bitterness often has a cause, although we don't know it at this stage in the novella.

AO1: Personal response: The reader is curious to discover exactly why Scrooge is bitter. The description is extreme, as few people bitterer than the bitterest wind in London.

AO2: The writer's effect: The writer has effectively compared Scrooge to a bitter wind. This implies that is natural that Scrooge to behave in this way, but like the wind there must be a cause for it.

AO3: Context: not applicable

3. 'They [rain, snow, hail, and sleet] often "came down" handsomely, and Scrooge never did' (34) - this shows that he is mean. He's not even as generous as bad weather, which is an extremely unfavourable comparison, making Scrooge appear to be a misanthropist even this early in the novella.

AO1: Personal response: the reader may feel that Scrooge is a misanthropist, unable to give anything of himself to others. This makes him an outsider in every sense of the word.

AO2: The writer's effect: through the use of natural imagery the writer is effectively showing Scrooge in a negative light.

He is far worse than anything the elements can throw at mankind in Victorian London.

AO3: Context: although the weather may not have been much worse during Victorian times than now, some poor people living on the street would have suffered greatly during times of bad weather. Additionally, some poor people's homes were inadequately equipped to deal with cold snaps. Even Bob Cratchit doesn't have enough coal on his fire in Scrooge's office to keep him warm.

4. 'No beggars implored him to bestow a trifle' (34) - this shows that even people living on the fringes of society, like beggars, are afraid of speaking Scrooge. They see him as a different kind of outsider.

AO1: Personal response: the reader must feel that Scrooge is truly frightening, if even beggars, desperate to survive, struggle to muster the strength to ask him for money.

AO2: The writer's effect: the writer uses negative words like 'no' to show how appalling Scrooge's attitude and appearance is.

AO3: Context: these were the 'hungry 40s' of the 19th century. There were many people in desperate need of food, so Scrooge must've been fearful indeed if beggars were afraid to approach him.

5. 'No children asked him what it was o'clock' (34) - this shows that Scrooge is a little intimidating. He is too scary the children to even dare to ask a simple question.

AO1: Personal response: Scrooge is clearly an 'ogre' of sorts, which is a word used to describe in later in the story. The children are right to be scared of an unfriendly and perhaps powerful outsider to their society

AO2: The writer's effect: the writer is portraying Scrooge is a monster, at this point. Scaring children is the stuff Frankenstein's monster, so the writer is effectively using Gothic techniques to induce fear in the reader.

AO3: Context: Mary Shelley's Frankenstein had been re-printed in 1831, so it is highly likely that Dickens read it and perhaps consciously or subconsciously used ideas taken from it in his 1843 novella. Interestingly, Abel Magwitch and Pip in Dickens's Great Expectations (1861) seem to parody the relationship between creator and creation in Frankenstein.

6. 'Even blind men's dogs [...] With to their owners into doorways and courts; and then would wag their tails as though they said, "no eye at all is better than an evil eye, dark master!"' (34) - this shows that dogs have an instinctive dislike of Scrooge, and can feel the evil that emanates from him.

AO1: Personal response: the mention of the 'evil eye' really makes Scrooge appear to be inhumane. The reader can have little sympathy with him, at this point. This is in direct contrast to the sympathy felt for the blindmen, relying on their dogs to avoid the evil Scrooge.

AO2: The writer's effect: the writer has used a trusted animal, like a blind man's dog, to show how awful Scrooge is as a person. It also creates a certain amount of superstition, if one believes that animals can detect evil better than humans.

AO3: Context: not applicable.

Hopefully you can turn those notes into an essay, but still only half our work is done. We need now to turn to the entire novella to see what we can dig out about Scrooge being an outsider.

Once again I'm going to look for around six points to make, ensuring I get the maximum marks.

Details in the extract showing Scrooge as an outsider

1. Initially, Scrooge shows his contempt for society, by treating Bob Cratchit appallingly. Although Scrooge has a small fire, Bob's is even smaller. To keep warm in Scrooge's office, Bob must 'put on his white comforter' and try 'to warm himself at the candle' (35).

AO1: Personal response: this shows the awful predicament of somebody with lowly status in Victorian London. Bob is a victim and Scrooge is exploiting him by refusing to give his employee enough heat to work effectively. Clearly, Scrooge's behaviour is inhumane and the reader can have no sympathy with him.

AO2: The writer's effect: by showing the appalling conditions that Bob Cratchit has to work in, the writer is manipulating the readers emotions. At this stage, all the reader sympathy

lies with Bob. The metaphorical lack of heat ties in with Scrooge's cold demeanour.

AO3: Context: for Bob, keeping a job with low pay and poor conditions is far better than seeking refuge in the workhouse, where he would be separated from his family and treated even worse.

2. Scrooge shows his contempt for society's tradition of Christmas by replying 'Humbug' to his nephew, who has been wishing him a merry Christmas (35). Scrooge thinks that 'every idiot who goes about with "Merry Christmas" on his lips, should be boiled with his own pudding, and buried with the stake of holly through his heart' (36).

AO1: Personal response: Scrooge's extreme reaction to Fred's invitation to get in tune with the season shows us how unsociable Scrooge is. It is clear that Scrooge cares very little for other people's opinions.

AO2: The writer's effect: there is some alliteration in Scrooge's speech, which emphasises its cruelty and its extreme views. The words 'boiled', 'buried', 'holly' and 'heart' are particularly noticeable to the reader. Additionally, holly is associated with Christmas, as is pudding. Scrooge's misanthropic speech shows that he has a total disregard the Christmas and wants to turn it upside down. His violent suggestions portrayed him as a very unpleasant person to the reader.

AO3: Context: the idea that a misanthrope can be changed into a kinder person through supernatural intervention was already trialed by Dickens in *The Pickwick Papers* (1836). Dickens was very much in touch with the mood of the times, and Prince Albert's popularising of a Christmas tree in 1841 and the newly emerging Christmas cards must have had an effect on the writer. Dickens wanted to defy utilitarians, the new business classes and political economists who wanted to do away with Christmas. Scrooge represents these killjoys.

3. Scrooge shows a total disregard for the poor, reminding the charity collectors that there are 'workhouses' and 'prisons' where food can be obtained (38).

AO1: Personal response: the reader feels no sympathy for Scrooge, who is adamant that those that fall on hard times should cope without any intervention.

AO2: The writer's effect: the mention of the 'Poor Law' and 'the treadmill' shows the writer wants the reader to understand the ramifications of political policies.

AO3: Context: the treadmill was used for the punishment of the people in the workhouses and prisons. It also was functional, in that it provided water or moved grain. Dickens was opposed to the Poor Law Amendment Act of 1834, mentioned by Scrooge. The result of this act of Parliament was conditions in the workhouse became significantly worse. This was a deliberate ploy by the government to reduce the cost of poor relief. The theory was that people would choose to work for low wages, rather than resort to living in the workhouse, which would only be a harsh alternative to starvation. In the workhouse, food would be just about adequate, it would be strict discipline and families would be separated. No longer could people receive poor relief payments in their own homes. For some, it was simply starvation or the workhouse.

4. By collecting debts from people, Scrooge has become very unpopular, as we see when he witnesses a young couple's relief that his death in the future. Scrooge's demise means they will not have to pay back the next loan instalment immediately.

AO1: Personal response: although Scrooge has a legal right to pursue money that is owed to him, this scene shows how unpalatable his behaviour is. A decent young couple are struggling to pay him back and feel guilty for rejoicing in Scrooge's death. Once again, the reader sees what an antisocial character Scrooge is. After all, he could have renegotiated the loan with the young couple to avoid them experiencing such heartache.

AO2: The writer's effect: the husband's words that 'we may sleep tonight with light hearts, Caroline' shows how perturbed they have been that they are struggling to repay the debt (104). Caroline was even hoping that Scrooge would relent, and give them more time to pay back what they owe. Scrooge's death in the future ensures that they have some extra time.

AO3: Context: debt-collecting was a very sensitive subject to Dickens. His father was imprisoned for not repaying money he had borrowed on time when Dickens was just a child. Dickens's father served a three-month jail sentence as a result. Dickens clearly felt that money borrowers should be more lenient with their customers should they succumb to harder times.

5. Scrooge's ex-fiancee, Belle, leaves him because she says that he wants to pursue 'Gain' (65).

AO1: Personal response: Scrooge's sympathetic portrayal continues when we find him rejecting love in favour of money. In contrast, Belle produces a happy family as a 'comely matron' (67).

AO2: The writer's effect: the writer personifies 'gain' by capitalising it, showing how important it is for Scrooge.

AO3: Context: Dickens was of the mind that capitalism would work better if the workers were well looked after. He believed that exploitation and ill-treatment could lead to a bloody revolution, so he continually urged political leaders and businessmen to put people before profits to ensure harmony.

6. Scrooge is left alone at school, even for the Christmas holidays. His sister, Fan, tries to rescue him from his solitude.

AO1: Personal response: the reader feels some sympathy for Scrooge, who is left alone at school while others have gone home to their families for Christmas. While Scrooge is lucky to have an education, he has certainly been neglected. That explains a lot of his antisocial behaviour. Nevertheless his

kind sister, insists that 'home's like Heaven!' (60). This shows his father is had a change of heart, but we do wonder how Scrooge has been treated prior to that.

AO2: The writer's effect: alliteration is used to emphasise how important the home is. The soft 'H' sound reminds the reader of how the young Scrooge must long for the creature comforts of home. Additionally, young Scrooge's home is compared to heaven, through the use of a simile. This adds religious significance, which is apt given the time of year.

AO3: Context: Dickens had already written in 1838 about the dangers of boarding schools, albeit those in Yorkshire. Clearly, Dickens was opposed to them, judging by the sentiments he voiced in *Nicholas Nickleby*.

Characters

Character names are very important. They often tell us a lot about the character we are about to encounter. Brainstorm words that come to mind, when you read character names. For instance, Scrooge may make you think of 'screw' and 'gouge', both of which have negative connotations. Do your words have negative connotations too? Try a different character and see what you come up with.

When you've finished that, draw the characters and label them based on the descriptions in the book. This will help embed important quotations should you get a question about characters.

Scrooge is such a memorable character that his name has even entered the English language to mean somebody who is mean with their money and reluctant to enjoy himself or herself. We discover that he is: 'a tight fisted hand grindstone' as well as 'a squeezing, wrenching, grasping, scraping, clutching, covetous old sinner!' (34). Physically his appearance shows him to have a 'pointed nose', a 'shrivelled' cheek, 'red' eyes, 'blue' and 'lips', a 'stiffened' gait, and a 'grating voice' (34). We also discover that he is cold enough to have 'a frosty rime' on his head and eyebrows, and 'a wiry chin' (34).

Adjectives that would describe Scrooge in the early part of the novella include the following: mean-spirited, cold-hearted, callous, and evil. The reformed Scrooge, of course, is completely different. This Scrooge is loving, kind, generous and above all happy, full of the joys of the season.

Bob Cratchit, meanwhile, can be described as passive and kind. He never changes during the novella, so he's little more than a caricature.

The same could be said of Tiny Tim. He may have been a stock character of Victorian fiction, but this portrayal of an innocent, passive disabled child can cause controversy today, with the Paralympics proving how disadvantages can be overcome.

Fred, unlike Scrooge in the early part of the novella, is jolly and good-natured.

Marley's ghost symbolises the monetary concerns in life. Similarly, the other ghosts are metaphors for Scrooge's life.

Themes

I will now briefly discuss some of the themes of the novella.

Greed - the idea that you cannot take your wealth to the grave is exemplified by Marley's ghost, who is chained by the monetary gains of the past. Scrooge has also suffered by his addiction to gain, although at the beginning of the novella he seems to have no regrets.

Poverty - the figures of 'Ignorance' and 'Want' come to mind, as do the Cratchit family, surviving below the poverty line. The message in this didactic novella is people are dying unnecessarily because of harsh conditions and poor pay at work. Luckily, the Tiny Tim, Scrooge's change of heart results in his survival.

Social life/community - through the characters of Fezziwig and Fred, we see how beneficial it can be to have parties and socialise. This kind of thing is completely absent from the life of Scrooge, who initially seems content to be alone.

Isolation - the message comes across the isolation is unhealthy, but younger Scrooge left alone at school had no choice. In later life, he is guilty of shunning humanity, but his lonely existence is more profitable than sharing his life with somebody.

Responsibility - clearly Dickens believes that rich people should take more responsibility for their poor employees, and to that end Scrooge eventually takes care of his poverty stricken clerk, Bob Cratchit.

Religion - Dickens believed that people should have the opportunity to enjoy recreational activities on Sundays should they so choose. The scene at the bakers shows us how much he disagreed with the Sabbatarian Movement.

Education - the fact that we are warned that 'Ignorance' is more dangerous than 'Want' tells us that education is a priority for Dickens. His involvement in Ragged Schools adds to that impression.

Supernatural - Dickens was a big believer in the power of the supernatural. He went to great lengths to explain that 'spontaneous combustion' could actually happen in the right set of circumstances. He also believed in mesmerism.

Imagination - Dickens also believed the power of the imagination could set people free and make them feel happier. The younger Scrooge is seen metaphorically devouring novels in much the way that Dickens did.

Structure

Should the question allow it, mentioning how Dickens's novella conforms to the narrative structure expected may get you additional marks. It is important that you mention that the fact that Jacob Marley is dead is the **precipitating action** of the novella, effectively pushing the story forward.

The visitations of the four ghosts, results in **rising action**. In other words, the story is becoming more intense at this point.

Then we have the typical **reversal**, as Scrooge refuses to look at the face of the dead man being robbed of all his worldly possessions. As readers, we feel pretty sure that it is in fact Scrooge was dead.

The **climax** comes thereafter, as the gravestone reveals Scrooge's name. This is the high point dramatically of the novel.

What follows is **falling action**, as we see a reformed Scrooge performing acts of kindness. Of course, there is less drama in this section.

Finally, we get the **resolution**, whereby we find out that Tiny Tim has survived after all.

Essay writing tips

Use a variety of connectives

Have a look of this list of connectives. Which of these would you choose to use?

'ADDING' DISCOURSE MARKERS

- AND
- ALSO
- AS WELL AS
- MOREOVER
- TOO
- FURTHERMORE
- ADDITIONALLY

I hope you chose 'additionally', 'furthermore' and 'moreover'. Don't be afraid to use the lesser discourse markers, as they are also useful. Just avoid using those ones over and over again. I've seen essays from Key Stage 4 students that use the same discourse marker for the opening sentence of each paragraph! Needless to say, those essays didn't get great marks!

Okay, here are some more connectives for you to look at. Select the best ones.

'SEQUENCING' DISCOURSE MARKERS

- NEXT
- FIRSTLY
- SECONDLY

- THIRDLY

- FINALLY

- MEANWHILE

- AFTER

- THEN

- SUBSEQUENTLY

This time, I hope you chose 'subsequently' and 'meanwhile'.

Here are some more connectives for you to 'grade'!

'ILLUSTRATING / EXEMPLIFYING' DISCOURSE MARKERS

- FOR EXAMPLE

- SUCH AS

- FOR INSTANCE

- IN THE CASE OF

- AS REVEALED BY

- ILLUSTRATED BY

I'd probably go for 'illustrated by' or even 'as exemplified by' (which is not in the list!). Please feel free to add your own examples to the lists. Strong connectives impress examiners. Don't forget it! That's why I want you to look at some more.

'CAUSE & EFFECT' DISCOURSE MARKERS

- BECAUSE

- SO

- THEREFORE

- THUS

- CONSEQUENTLY

- HENCE

I'm going for 'consequently' this time. How about you? What about the next batch?

'COMPARING' DISCOURSE MARKERS

- SIMILARLY

- LIKEWISE

- AS WITH

- LIKE

- EQUALLY

- IN THE SAME WAY

I'd choose 'similarly' this time. Still some more to go.

'QUALIFYING' DISCOURSE MARKERS

- BUT

- HOWEVER

- WHILE

- ALTHOUGH

- UNLESS

- EXCEPT

- APART FROM

- AS LONG AS

It's 'however' for me!

'CONTRASTING' DISCOURSE MARKERS

- WHEREAS

- INSTEAD OF

- ALTERNATIVELY

- OTHERWISE

- UNLIKE

- ON THE OTHER HAND

- CONVERSELY

I'll take 'conversely' or 'alternatively' this time.

'EMPHASISING' DISCOURSE MARKERS

- ABOVE ALL

- IN PARTICULAR

- ESPECIALLY

- SIGNIFICANTLY

- INDEED

- NOTABLY

You can breathe a sigh of relief now! It's over! No more connectives. However, now I want to put our new found skills to use in our essays.

Useful information/Glossary

Allegory: extended metaphor, like the grim reaper representing death, e.g. Scrooge symbolizing capitalism.

Alliteration: same consonant sound repeating, e.g. 'She sells sea shells'.

Allusion: reference to another text/person/place/event.

Ascending tricolon: sentence with three parts, each increasing in power, e.g. 'ringing, drumming, shouting'.

Aside: character speaking so some characters cannot hear what is being said. Sometimes, an aside is directly to the audience. It's a dramatic technique which reveals the character's inner thoughts and feelings.

Assonance: same vowel sounds repeating, e.g. 'Oh no, won't Joe go?'

Bathos: abrupt change from sublime to ridiculous for humorous effect.

Blank verse: lines of unrhymed iambic pentameter.

Compressed time: when the narrative is fast-forwarding through the action.

Descending tricolon: sentence with three parts, each decreasing in power, e.g. 'shouting, talking, whispering'.

Denouement: tying up loose ends, the resolution.

Diction: choice of words or vocabulary.

Didactic: used to describe literature designed to inform, instruct or pass on a moral message.

Dilated time: opposite compressed time, here the narrative is in slow motion.

Direct address: second person narrative, predominantly using the personal pronoun 'you'.

Dramatic action verb: manifests itself in physical action, e.g. I punched him in the face.

Dramatic irony: audience knows something that the character is unaware of.

Ellipsis: leaving out part of the story and allowing the reader to fill in the narrative gap.

End-stopped lines: poetic lines that end with punctuation.

Epistolary: letter or correspondence-driven narrative.

Flashback/Analepsis: going back in time to the past, interrupting the chronological sequence.

Flashforward/Prolepsis: going forward in time to the future, interrupting the chronological sequence.

Foreshadowing/Adumbrating: suggestion of plot developments that will occur later in the narrative.

Gothic: another strand of Romanticism, typically with a wild setting, a sensitive heroine, an older man with a 'piercing gaze', discontinuous structure, doppelgangers, guilt and the 'unspeakable' (according to Eve Kosofsky Sedgwick).

Hamartia: character flaw, leading to that character's downfall.

Hyperbole: exaggeration for effect.

Iambic pentameter: a line of ten syllables beginning with a lighter stress alternating with a heavier stress in its perfect form, which sounds like a heartbeat. The stress falls on the even syllables, numbers: 2, 4, 6, 8 and 10, e.g. 'When now I think you can behold such sights'.

Intertextuality: links to other literary texts.

Irony: amusing or cruel reversal of expected outcome or words meaning the opposite to their literal meaning.

Metafiction/Romantic irony: self-conscious exposure of the devices used to create 'the truth' within a work of fiction.

Motif: recurring image use of language or idea that connects the narrative together and creates a theme or mood, e.g. 'green light' in *The Great Gatsby.*

Oxymoron: contradictory terms combined, e.g. deafening silence.

Pastiche: imitation of another's work.

Pathetic fallacy: a form of personification whereby inanimate objects show human attributes, e.g. 'the sea smiled benignly'. The originator of the term, John Ruskin in 1856, used 'the cruel, crawling foam', from Kingsley's *The Sands of Dee*, as an example to clarify what he meant by the 'morbid' nature of pathetic fallacy.

Personification: concrete or abstract object made human, often simply achieved by using a capital letter or a personal pronoun, e.g. 'Nature', or describing a ship as 'she'.

Pun/Double entendre: a word with a double meaning, usually employed in witty wordplay but not always.

Retrospective: account of events after they have occurred.

Romanticism: genre celebrating the power of imagination, spriritualism and nature.

Semantic/lexical field: related words about a single concept, e.g. king, queen and prince are all concerned with royalty.

Soliloquy: character thinks aloud, but is not heard by other characters (unlike in a monologue) giving the audience access to inner thoughts and feelings.

Style: choice of language, form and structure, and effects produced.

Synecdoche: one part of something referring to the whole, e.g. Carker's teeth represent him in *Dombey and Son*.

Syntax: the way words and sentences are placed together.

Tetracolon climax: sentence with four parts, culminating with the last part, e.g. 'I have nothing to offer but blood, toil, tears, and sweat ' (Winston Churchill).

ABOUT THE AUTHOR

Joe Broadfoot is a secondary school teacher of English and a soccer journalist, who also writes fiction and literary criticism. His former experiences as a DJ took him to far-flung places such as Tokyo, Kobe, Beijing, Hong Kong, Jakarta, Cairo, Dubai, Cannes, Oslo, Bergen and Bodo. He is now PGCE and CELTA-qualified with QTS, a first-class honours degree in Literature and an MA in Victorian Studies (majoring in Charles Dickens). Drama is close to his heart as he acted in 'Macbeth' and 'A Midsummer Night's Dream' at the Royal Northern College of Music in Manchester. More recently, he has been teaching 'Much Ado About Nothing' to 'A' Level students at a secondary school in Buckinghamshire, 'An Inspector Calls' at a school in west London and 'Heroes' at a school in Kent.

CPSIA information can be obtained at www.ICGtesting.com
Printed in the USA
LVOW10s0157270216

476862LV00026BA/772/P